Dr. Freud, Fish Whisperer

With heartfelt thanks to Ferdinand Scherrer
M. M.-C.

To all the adorable fish who think along with me
N. N.

Dr. Freud, Fish Whisperer

Narrated by
Marion Muller-Colard

Illustrated by
Nathalie Novi

Translated by
Anna Street

Plato & Co.
diaphanes

Dr. Freud stares out of his window at the gray sky.
The apartment at 19, Berggasse is too large. Or perhaps it is too small. Yes, that's it. The apartment is too small, muses the doctor as he loosens his collar. And Vienna. The city of Vienna is too small. Not to mention the world! The human mind. Bingo! The human mind is too small. Unless it is too large.

"Will it rain?" the doctor murmurs under his breath, trying to stick to tangible things.

Ever since he came back from Paris a few years ago, he dreads the mood swings of the Viennese spring.

I should nevertheless go for a walk, "to clear my mind," as the French say. But the doctor, who has recently written an article on the anatomy of the brain, knows better than anyone that it's a very bad sign to have one's brain actually exposed to the open air.

"It's just an expression," reassures Professor Charcot, always a bit amused by his young Austrian student's tendency to take everything seriously. "Relax, my dear Sigmund! No one has the intention of opening your skull and stretching out your mind. It's a figure of speech, if you prefer."

Sigmund Freud did prefer, as a matter of fact.

“Figure of speech or not, I for my part most certainly have the intention of stretching all the minds in the world!”

Yet despite the young student’s efforts to dissect the gray matter, connect synapses and scrutinize the cortex, the brain opened out like an accordion: immediately folding back upon itself into strange, musical patterns that were new every time. Sometimes, at night, Dr. Freud dreams he is lost inside the human brain, trying to find his way out of the labyrinth of cerebral convolutions. He implores all the gods of mythology to toss him a life line, such as Ariadne’s thread. “Useless,” he echoes repeatedly.

“I feel too small,” he finally announces, glancing at a picture of his teacher hanging on the wall in his study.

It shows Professor Charcot holding a hypnotized patient in his arms. Must patients be put to sleep for them to be able to say, as though in a dream, what makes them unwell? Sometimes, it works. Other times, it doesn’t. Are there no other ways of opening the mind?

Figure of speech...

Dr. Freud hears the voice of Professor Charcot in his head... And what if Charcot didn’t have the last word? Dr. Freud slams the door to his study, making the paintings on the wall and the famous picture tremble...

As he slips on his shoes for an outdoor stroll, he gets tangled up by all the knots in his laces. He suddenly thinks of his old fishing pole, forgotten at the back of the hallway closet.

"I'll go fishing!" he exclaims with glee, jumping up and down like a child. "It's been such a long time!"

And so off goes Dr. Freud on his way to the lake, his fishing pole swung over his shoulder.

When walking, one thinks differently. When fishing, it's something else again. Dr. Freud always liked to wonder about the different ways people think.

"We do not think like a frog hopping from one lily pad to another," he muses while watching a batrachian frolic upon the water's surface.

He unrolls the reel of his fishing pole to give his line some slack.

"That's exactly it," he says, smiling to himself. "We think like we unroll a fishing line. Our ideas are all linked to one another."

And he tosses his float farther out into the lake, there where the bank drops off and gives way to the depths.

"You, for example, your laces made you think of your fishing pole."

Dr. Freud looks all around, petrified.

"Who said that?"

It seems as if the voice is coming from the circular ripples made by the float bobbing in the water.

“No matter,” replies the voice. “What matters is what you just said! Do you realize what it means? It supposes that what I think today goes back, from one end of the fishing line to the other, to my very first thought!”

Silence hangs over the lake. Dr. Freud scans the surface creased with ripples. But he cannot tell the gray sky from the gray water. Where is the line of separation, and from where comes the voice? From his lily pad, a green frog jumps into the water with a croak.

“And how far back does my very first thought go?” asks the small voice.

“That is a very big question,” sighs Dr. Freud who has suddenly forgotten that he doesn’t know whom he is talking to.

In the middle of the lake, the fishing rod’s float starts to sink.

“In the name of a codfish, I have a bite!” exclaims Dr. Freud.

“By Jove it bites,” adds the strange small voice, sounding as though it had something stuck between its teeth...

Dr. Freud pulls on his line and brings up a fine, seven-pound carp.

“Woohoo! Nice catch,” he remarks, licking his chops.

He wades into the water to unhook the fish dangling from the line.

"And so, small voice, what do you think of that?"

But there is no reply. In Dr. Freud's hands, the carp moves its lips, mute. She looks up at him without struggling. With a little urging, she would gut herself and arrange herself sensibly on the dinner plates of the Freud family. He loosens his grip and holds the fish flat in his hands:

"Go on then, jump back in," he finally whispers.
"Why don't you save yourself?"

And he leans over and slips it back into the water. To his big surprise, the carp swims back and rubs against his hand.

Intrigued, Dr. Freud comments, "You seem like a very complicated carp."

"It felt good to be in your hands."

Is the small voice speaking to Dr. Freud coming from the carp?

"Holy mackerel! That's impossible," reasons Dr. Freud.
"A carp is mute... Fish don't speak!"

"If you are right, then that leaves only one other possibility: you can hear even what is unsaid."

Stupefied, Dr. Freud sits down in the water without realizing it. He drops his head into his hands then wipes his glasses which he needs to be able to see. Why did he put the carp back into the water? Did he really want it to live, this fish that is so willing to die?

Dr. Freud rummages in the algae looking for the carp.

"I think it is going through a bout of fish depression..."

Dr. Freud can't stand for anything depressed to pass through his hands without his understanding why. Once more, he dreams of the porthole through which he will find the knot in the brain that drives people to let themselves go off the deep end. Or that drives melancholic carps to let themselves be fished out...

Dr. Freud rolls up his sleeves and plunges in search of the small voice that lures him towards the bottom.

He doesn't need to swim very far, it looks as though the carp is waiting for him right in front of the algae. Sometimes he can see her, and sometimes she stays hidden. But he can always hear her:

"Are you taking me back with you?" asks the carp, curious.

"Why the devil are you so bent on getting caught!?"

"I prefer to die in your hands than to live alone in these cold waters," says the carp. "And you, why did you let me go? You who were so bent on bringing fish back to the house?"

"It was a subconsciously deliberate act. . . Perhaps I don't like fish as much as I thought I did. Perhaps I knew you had something to teach me?"

The carp feels flattered. She quivers more than ever, making the strangest faces.

"Why are you twisting your mouth like that?"

"I have a terrible toothache," the carp answers.
"I think the tip of your hook is stuck in my mouth."

An inner wound – this is most definitely a mission for Dr. Freud. Conveniently, the carp finally offers:

"Would you like to see my home?"

Dr. Freud hesitates. Lately he attempts to have his patients lie down on a divan to make them talk. It's an experiment... but a fish lying on its back would not exactly be a sign of positive vitality. And so, when the carp holds out her fin to Dr. Freud, he grabs it and lets himself be drawn into the deep...

Dr. Freud and the carp swim in silence side by side for a long time. They thread their way through strands of algae. Soon, the rays of light that pierce the lake like so many warm fingers no longer reach them.

Suddenly, the carp makes a sharp U-turn. The way she swipes her tail left and right seems intended to bar her visitor's passage.

"What's the matter, Carp?" the visitor asks, intrigued.

The carp moves her lips but her voice is once again mute.

"I think you're blushing..."

At these words, the carp blushes even more.

"I'm so ashamed, so ashamed! I'm ashamed to blush,
I'm afraid of..."

The words come bursting out like bubbles rising to the surface.

Dr. Freud knits his brows. He would like to be able to light one of his cigars which always help him think. But damp tobacco will never burn.

"You are not ashamed to blush, but you blush because you are ashamed, is that it?"

The carp nods. She doesn't say another word. The back of her mouth still hurts

Dr. Freud finds this question of shame very interesting. Isn't it shame that so often paralyzes his patients? To be honest, doesn't shame paralyze himself as well from time to time?

Trying, this time, to offer the carp a helping hand rather than a fishing hook, Dr. Freud gently asks, "And what troubles you so much that you can't tell me about your shame?"

But the fish remains silent.

Dr. Freud ruminates. He strokes his beard as though to rub out the knots creating an obstruction between himself and the carp. He would like the fish to let him through...

"You know," he says with a yawn to give the impression that it is really of no importance, "shame never transformed a carp into a goldfish."

The carp's eyes light up.

"Even with your shame, you can still be you. As for me with my shame, I can still be me. And if I feel my own shame, I can certainly see yours without judging it."

The carp's scales seem to shine again.

The carp takes Dr. Freud's hand once more and leads him a little further on into the deep. Arriving at the very bottom, the fish sinks into the sludge. Only her eyes stick out from the swampy mud at the bottom of the lake.

"This is my home," says the carp in a quiet voice.
"You can see how dirty it is."

"It's not dirty, it's dark. It is hard to see very well..."

"But I prefer it like this."

"You prefer not being able to see clearly?" repeats Dr. Freud as he pulls a small notebook from his pocket. He likes to keep a record of enigmas and discoveries.

With her mouth pursed tightly, the carp utters no denial. Discreetly, Dr. Freud jots down in his notebook:

Shame = Sludge
Dark place = Prefers not seeing clearly

"Eureka!" he reflects suddenly. "It all makes sense! If someone is ashamed, he will hide his shame in a secret, private place where no one can judge him! He will bury it in the sludge and..."

But something doesn't jibe... The carp should have left her shame there in the sludge and gone back up to live her life on the surface! No one, not even a fish, can stand to stew in one's shame forever...

The carp is sinking even deeper into the sludge. Pretty soon, even her eyes will be covered. Something must be done, quickly!

"She is ashamed in front of me," Dr. Freud supposes. "What if I stay behind her back? What if she cannot see me? What if I speak very softly, like a voice inside her head... Perhaps it will then be easier for her to speak."

Passing slowly around the fish, Dr. Freud sits down behind it on a little rock jutting up out of the sludge.

"What surprises me," he ventures in a monotonous voice, "is that you bit the hook..."

Is the carp ever going to take Dr. Freud's bait this time? After a few minutes, the sludge at the bottom of the lake begins to murmur.

"I don't know... The little hook caught my eye, sparkling above me. It was shining like the ring you wear on your finger... so I wanted to swallow it."

Dr. Freud looks at the wedding ring on his finger. He has been married to Martha for five years now. He thinks about his wedding day. He thinks about his oldest daughter, Mathilda, who is almost four years old and wants to climb up on his lap all the time. His thoughts undulate like algae as he rambles. Stop daydreaming, Dr. Freud says, as he snaps back and tries to concentrate. Quite clearly, with this carp, something fishy is going on.

"And you weren't afraid of dying when you bit the hook?"

"Oh..." the carp sighs softly.
"I thought it might be easier, if I were dead."

"Our souls are warped," Dr. Freud thought.

In his short life, he had already heard enough to realize that everyone is full of contradictions. Everyone wants nothing more than to live, yet all the while running straight towards death!

"Death certainly makes things simpler. But it also makes them a lot less interesting," he says in an attempt to draw his melancholic carp out of the mud.

The fish seems insensitive to philosophical reasoning. In fact, she appears to be downright indifferent to everything in general.

"Death drive—the case is actually quite serious then," Dr. Freud says to himself.

He rolls up his sleeves and writes *"Thanatos"* in his notebook. He likes using Greek words. They give the impression of meaning more than ordinary words. Like beacons lighting up the dark crevasses inaccessible to humans. *Thanatos* represents not only death that comes when one stops breathing. It is the way death seeps into life, invading the world of the living with the power to break life's momentum. It is similar in this way to the word Eros. Eros does not merely refer to the love between two people who decide to love each other. It also refers to something much stronger than choice, to a kind of volcano, an irrepressible desire to touch someone and to belong to that person entirely. That or die.

"Eros, Thanatos. Thanatos, Eros," Dr. Freud repeats, barely moving his lips.

He jumbles the two words so quickly in his head that in the end, he can't tell them apart. It takes him a moment to realize that the carp just said something that reveals much more than she could have possibly imagined.

"Your voice sounds like my daddy's voice," the carp has just said.

Eros and *Thanatos*, whirling around in Dr. Freud's head, violently collide.

"You have the same moustache as well. My daddy was quite good-looking."

Dr. Freud blushed. He'd never had such a nice compliment from a fish. Well, to be frank, he'd never had any kind of compliment at all from a fish. He nonetheless notices that the carp talks about her daddy in the past tense.

"Why do you say he *was* good-looking. Is he gone?"

"I don't know," says the carp. "I don't know what happened to him..."

"Holy codfish!" Dr. Freud remarks to himself, "this missing dad business is one big catch. Haven't the poets always said, in their own way, that childhood leaves lasting marks on all of us? But what can help the carp to fish up her old memories? It all seems so long ago, so far away, so deep within..."

Dr. Freud looks at his feet which are sinking into the mud. There is no end to sinking, he thinks. Suddenly, it seems to him that some underground world is displaying strange images at his feet. In places, the mud loses its opacity and one can see straight through, similar to the bottom of the mountain lakes he visited as a child. One proud little boy learnt to swim in those waters.

"Do you remember what I was saying back on the embankment?" Dr. Freud asks softly, a bit hypnotized by the glittering images. "About the history of our thoughts that unroll like a fishing line? You were certainly right when you said that if we retrace our line of thought, we can find our way back to our very first thoughts..."

Dr. Freud lets his words float to the gills of the carp. Then he continues:

"And what if the two of us were to follow this line? Figure of speech, of course..."

A deafening silence blows like a wind through the bottom of the lake. Dr. Freud feels his feet sink deeper into the sludge as though caught in quicksand. Will he make it back to the small child he saw earlier?

The carp, in front of him, has a mouth full of mud from moving her lips without saying a word. It was in the hands of Dr. Freud that she remembered her daddy. But all the rest gets bogged down in unfamiliar, dark waters. How can one remember what one has forgotten?

So the carp grabs hold of the line Dr. Freud holds out. A line with a little circle of silver at the end.

"It was shining above me," repeats the carp.
"I had never seen anything so shiny...
Well, actually, yes I had, once. It was... it was Mommy's ring.
Mommy... she wore a wedding ring on her fin and..."

But the train of memories suddenly seems to break off.
Dr. Freud has taken off his wedding ring in order to have a better look at it. On the inside is engraved his wife's name, Martha. And the date, September 13, 1886.

During this time, the carp's lips move in silence. Mud surges into her mouth which hurts. Is it really a piece of the hook? Upon reflection, the carp's mouth already hurt before that. Before she bit Dr. Freud's hook... But when she speaks, the mud comes back out, when she speaks, it doesn't hurt as much. Hold on to the line. Wedding ring, Mommy, sludge.
Yes, here it is, the line leads back to that.

"One day, Mommy's wedding ring slipped off. We were at the surface, swallowing insects. We saw the ring sink to the bottom. Daddy rushed to catch it, but he was still far away when the ring disappeared into the middle of the algae.

We searched for a long time, the three of us. Mommy cried a lot. When night began to fall, Daddy took Mommy by the fin and tried to convince her to return to the hollow log where we slept. Right when Daddy and Mommy turned to swim back home, I saw something sparkle in the sludge.

I watched my parents swim away, holding fins.
I resented Mommy, I don't know why. I resented her because Daddy was thinking only of her and of how upset she was.
And so... instead of giving her the ring, I swallowed it.
So that she would never find it again."

Dr. Freud wrote everything down. At the same time, his attention wandered... under his feet in the water danced the folds of a dress belonging to Amalia, his own mother. A tent-like dress under which one could take cover. The young Sigmund had a hard time admitting that six more children after he came out from under that skirt. Wasn't he precious little Sigi, her golden child? The others were fake, made of rubbish, so there!

Stung by an old jealousy, Dr. Freud rolls his wedding ring between his fingers. Martha, September 13, 1886. This is typical of wedding rings: the husband wears the name of his wife on his ring, and the wife wears the name of her husband on hers.

How much time will go by before all this comes together in Dr. Freud's mind? The notes in his notebook create a whirlpool in which his thoughts and his own memories get tangled up with the carp's story.

The Greeks had already written it all down with the story of Oedipus Rex: little boys are in love with their mother and see their father as a rival. Little girls are in love with their father and... This is why the carp swallowed her mommy's wedding ring, he muses. She wanted to have her precious daddy all to herself.

No need to dissect anyone's brain: all one needs to do is listen to the patients! They always tell the pure and simple truth... each in their own way of speaking.

Dr. Freud jumps at this discovery and the carp gives a little cough. Moving her fins, she tries to push back the sludge which is closing over her.

The fish really needs to get out of this mess, Dr. Freud says to himself. Should he tell her the story of Oedipus Rex? It might be a bit too much for a fish. So Dr. Freud keeps Oedipus to himself – he can always write a book about it later. For the time being, he comes back to the carp and holds out his hand.

"Long before you were born, I knew that a little carp who loved her daddy so much that she swallowed her mommy's wedding ring would come to me..."

"Do you talk with the good Lord in order to know everything in advance?"

Dr. Freud smiles. The carp puts her fin in his hand and pulls herself a bit further out of the mud.

"I had forgotten all of that," she says, shaking her scales. "All the same, I am a little ashamed..."

"We forget what is painful to us... what frightens us, what distresses or humiliates us... It is perfectly normal, my dear carp, that you buried all that deep in the sludge."

Her mouth still hurts a little, but the carp seems ready to follow Dr. Freud to the surface . .

Suddenly, they hear some hollering.

“Ribbit me ribbit. No way is Id getting up on my lily pad, forget it!”

“Um, well I, uh... I don’t know. I can let Id come up on my lily pad...” hesitates a tiny voice..

“Croak my heart and hope to die, if you do that, I’ll poke your eye.”

Dr. Freud looks up towards the surface. He sees a frog trying in vain to jump out of the water. Each time he tries, another frog gives him a furious kick, plunging him back into the water.

“They’re at it again!” laughs the carp.

“Do you know them?” asks Dr. Freud, intrigued.

With their eyes just under the surface, Dr. Freud and the carp look towards the bobbing water lilies.

"They do this every day," sighs the carp. "Id tries to climb up on his lily pad, *Super-Ego* slaps him down, *Id* retreats, and *Ego* gets all upset."

"How very interesting," comments Dr. Freud, furiously sketching and taking notes. "Are those really their names?"

"One of them is called *Id*. The mean one is called *Super-Ego* and the hesitant one is called *Ego*," explains the carp, finding Dr. Freud a bit slow on the uptake.

A few lily pads away, the quarrel starts up again:
"*Id* has no business being here! *Id* must stay in the sludge. I did warn everyone!" *Super-Ego* insists in a bossy tone.
"*Id* is not even a frog: he is a croak between a frog and a creature from the abyss... What comes from the abyss stays in the abyss!" she mutters angrily with a booming voice.

Id manages to bring his head up out of the water:

"But why – ribbit – why?" he asks before being sent flying back underwater by his fellow creature's stomping foot.

"*Id* doesn't even croak like us..."

"All I said is just that perhaps *Id* belongs with us..."
Ego timidly suggests.

"Oh yeah? Over my dead body!"

"What do you have against your frog friend, in the end?" finally asks the carp who had swum up closer to the two frogs.

"*Id* is not a frog," replied the first one with a disgusted look.

"Well for what it's worth, I say... that he is a little bit frog all the same, isn't he?" shoots back the second one.

"No way! Id always tries to look between our legs. He doesn't behave at all like a polite frog."

"Well then, we could say that he is a frog, but an impolite frog," concludes the wavering voice with increasing assurance.

The carp swims back to Dr. Freud who has hoisted himself up on a rock where he continues taking notes with much concentration.

"This is fantastic!" he finally exclaims.

Dr. Freud shows his notes to the carp and enthusiastically explains:

"What is happening between the frogs is exactly what happens in each one of us, my dear carp!"

With wide eyes, the carp, flabbergasted, stays at the surface to listen to Dr. Freud.

"We all have an Id that wants to look between the legs... or under mommy's skirts," continues Dr. Freud, thinking of the young Sigi he used to be... "And a Super-Ego who teaches us that such things are forbidden when one is a child! And so Id, ashamed, is repressed into the sludge..."

"And Ego, in the middle, who doesn't know whom to believe... all this ties our brain up in virtual knots, to be sure..."

"Exactly!" cries Dr. Freud delightedly, overjoyed to have found such a clever disciple.

The carp finds all this fishinating. As for Dr. Freud, he understands that the psychology of the depths he just discovered in the lake was nothing other than the psychology of the mind.

"The main thing is that 'this doesn't stop something from existing,' as my dear Professor Charcot would say..."

Suddenly, the carp begins to wince and cough. She finally coughs up the little piece wedged at the back of her mouth: a wedding ring! Her mommy's wedding ring. Dr. Freud catches it and holds it up.

"It seems that you couldn't keep this one down!"

The carp quivers with immense relief. She is going to be able to go home and give the ring back to her mother. One day, she will get married as well. And her husband will become a perfect daddy for all their little baby fish.

"I guess we could say that all this gave us something to chew on," jokes the carp.

"Figure of speech," Dr. Freud and the carp say in unison, with knowing smiles.

The day is beginning to wane. Dr. Freud leaps from his rock back to the embankment. The carp swims up to him.

“Are you leaving then?” asks the carp, sticking her head up through water’s surface.

“I have work to do, I must get back...”

“And will you remember me?”

On the bank, Dr. Freud dries off with uncanny speed.

“Of course I will remember you!”

The carp seems reassured.

“Stay a bit longer, tell me another story!”

“But soon it will be dark... you won’t be able to see me anymore.”

“That doesn’t matter,” says the carp. “When you talk, everything becomes clear...”

This day, let's agree to call it Sigmund Freud's *carpe diem*.
It is, in a way, the day Dr. Freud discovered psychoanalysis.

"The surest way to straighten out the mind is to follow the line of thought," he muses as he watches the carp swim away into the dark waters. "Figure of speech..."

He reels his fishing line back up. When he gets to the hook, he gazes at the little bent piece.

"Figure of speech!" he calls out to an elderly man fishing next to him who doesn't seem to have noticed any of Dr. Freud's water ballet. "Our figure of speech, here, is the hook that will fish up what we have repressed from the surface of our consciousness!"

The old fisherman shrugs his shoulders indifferently.
As for Dr. Freud, he tells himself that an entire life will never be long enough to explore the vast reaches of the human psyche.

Back at home, he puts away his scalpel and decides that he will never need to use it again.

Today, Sigmund Freud has grown old. Even his divan is getting worn out. He is exhausting himself writing an article entitled "Analysis Terminable and Interminable."

"Muddy subject," he sighs despite himself.

He meant to say, "massive subject," but his tongue, which tricks him all the time, had tricked him again. Will it ever be possible to get to the bottom of the human subconscious? Dr. Freud admits that there is always, in the sludge's hollow, a protruding rock, a "corner-stone" that no speech can break open.

Furiously, he jots down this strange impression... Sometimes in psychoanalysis, one has the impression of "preaching to the fish."

Preaching to the fish, what a funny expression, Sigmund Freud muses, slouching over his desk. Why did he write that? He remembers a poem by Saint Anthony of Padua, which his friend Gustav Mahler had put to music...

The third movement of his Symphony No. 2...
"With quietly flowing movement..."

But as for Dr. Freud's thoughts, they stopped short like the spring tides caught in a flood lock.

Of all that he'd learned over the years, Dr. Freud never forgot one important thing: dreams are the best way to find the line once it has been lost. To this end, a little nap can't do any harm.

Lying down on his couch, Dr. Freud's eyelids close like tramway doors. He arrives in the entryway where he trips on a line. He almost falls but a big fish suddenly appears and catches him.

"Do you remember me?" asks a small voice.

"Well..." Dr. Freud strokes his beard as he ruminates. "Aren't you... the carp? The carp of the famous *carpe diem?*"

The carp grabs Dr. Freud's hands in her fins and starts spinning with him, round and round. Dr. Freud roars with laughter:

"Oh my dear carp. How happy I am to see you in my old age! Would you like to see the rest of the house?"

The carp doesn't wait but slips into Dr. Freud's office and glances through his work.

"Oh my, you wrote about me?" she asks, reading the strange line Dr. Freud had just written.

Dr. Freud blushes. He doesn't know what to say. He had written about "preaching to the fish" in a rather irritated tone.

"It's a figure of speech," he says apologetically.

"Come on... you and me, we know very well that everything is a figure of speech..."

"The interesting thing," the carp suggests as she unwinds a line that she is pulling from Dr. Freud's mouth, "would be to understand why you wrote that instead of something else."

Dr. Freud, exhausted, heads toward his couch to lie down. As he closes his eyes, he hums his old friend Mahler's tune, repeating the words of Saint Anthony of Padua:

St. Anthony arrives for his Sermon
and finds the church empty.
He goes to the rivers
to preach to the fishes;
They flick their tails,
which glisten in the sunshine.
The carp with roe
have all come here,
their mouths wide open,
listening attentively.
No sermon ever
pleased the carp so.
The sermon having ended,
each turns himself around;
The sermon has pleased them,
but they remain the same as before.

"This is the disappointment," sighs Dr. Freud at the end of his song… "My patients all remain as they were before!"

"Well, you see, with me, that's what I liked. I'm quite happy to have stayed a carp," murmurs the fish as she fades away. "A talking carp…"

When Dr. Freud opens his eyes, the first thing he sees is a little crack in the ceiling. Do all his patients stare at this white, cracked ceiling as they lie here?

"What did I dream?" he asks, running his fingers through his beard.

He sits back down on the couch and rubs his eyes.

Suddenly, he sees a shadow slip out through the half-open door. Like the silhouette of a fish swimming out into the deep.

“A talking carp,” he hears as in an echo.

Near the end of his life, Sigmund Freud tells himself that he is simply quite happy to have remained Sigmund Freud. Sigmund Freud, fish whisperer.

French edition
Marion Muller-Colard & Nathalie Novi
Le Professeur Freud parle aux poissons
Design: Yohanna Nguyen

With the kind support of

INSTITUT FRANÇAIS

First edition
ISBN 978-3-0358-0007-4

www.platoandco.net
www.diaphanes.com

Layout: 2edit, Zurich
Printed and bound in Germany